Luther O. Emerson

Cheerful Voices

A collection of songs, duets, trios and sacred pieces, for juvenile classes,

public schools and seminaries, to which is prefixed a complete and

attractive course of elementary instructions

Luther O. Emerson

Cheerful Voices
*A collection of songs, duets, trios and sacred pieces, for juvenile classes, public
schools and seminaries, to which is prefixed a complete and attractive course of
elementary instructions*

ISBN/EAN: 9783337384005

Printed in Europe, USA, Canada, Australia, Japan

Cover: Foto ©Thomas Meinert / pixelio.de

More available books at **www.hansebooks.com**

CHEERFUL VOICES

.. AND ..

SUNSHINE IN SONG

COMBINED.

A CHOICE COLLECTION OF BEAUTIFUL SONGS
FOR THE SCHOOL ROOM, INSTITUTES
AND SINGING CLASSES.

BY J. F. KING,

PRICE, PER DOZEN, $1.80; SINGLE COPY, 20c.
SPECIAL PRICE PER 100.

————————

J. F. KING, Publisher,
ORRVILLE, OHIO.

PREFACE.

Being encouraged by our GOLDEN THOUGHTS IN SONG, THE SILVER STAR, OUR PRIDE, and CRYSTAL CHIMES, published recently by us. we now present "CHEERFUL VOICES, for use in Public Schools, Institutes, and the Home Circle," etc. Music in the Public Schools has long since ceased to be an experiment. It is of service to a greater number of persons than any other art. The poorest get from it comfort and enjoyment, and the rich joy and peace. It may be so taught as to reach the foundation of the character, and the Common School is especially the place for teaching singing. That this volume may go forth bringing joy and peace to those who use it, and that it may brighten and broaden the life of our youth, is the wish of

THE AUTHOR.

GREETING SONG.

E. R. LATTA.

J. F. KINC.

Not too slow.

1. With a wel-come now we greet you, As we all as-sem-ble here,
2. It is pleasant thus to min-gle, And our voi-ces blend in song,
3. All our cares and all our trou-bles, What-co-ev-er ill be-tide,
4. We shall cher-ish pleasant mem'ries Of the joys this hour we know,

We have come with fa-ces smi-ling, And with spir-its full of cheer.
Thus we love each oth-er bet-ter, As we pass thro' life a-long.
While we min-gle here to-geth-er, Let us strive to lay a-side.
They will fall like sun-shine o'er us, As the sea-sons come and go.

CHORUS.

Welcome friends! with joy we meet you, Our's a welcome all sin-cere!

With the voice of song we greet you, With a welcome, welcome, welcome here.

Words used by per.

No. 2. LEARN A LITTLE EVERY DAY.

J. F. KING.

Cheerfully.

1. Lit - tle rills make wi-der streamlets, Streamlets swell the riv-er's flow,
2. Ti- ny seeds make plenteous har-vest, Drops of rain compose the show'rs,
3. Let us, while we read or stud - y, Cull a flow'r from ev- 'ry page,

Riv-ers join the mountain bil - lows, On-ward, on-ward as they go.
Seconds make the fly - ing minutes, And the minutes make the hours.
Here a line and there a precept, 'Gainst the lone-ly time of age.

Life is made of smallest fragments, Shade and sunshine, work and play,
Let us hast - en then and catch them, As they pass us on our way,
At our work or by the way - side, While we pon - der, while we play,

So may we, with greatest prof-it, Learn a lit - tle ev - 'ry day.
And with hon-est, true en-deav-or, Learn a lit - tle ev - 'ry day.
Let us then by con-stant ef-fort, Learn a lit - tle ev - 'ry day.

No. 3. MERRY WARBLERS.

LAURA E. NEWELL.   J. F. KING.

1. Mer-ry warblers, hap-py warblers, Light-ly swinging on the bough,
2. Car-ol soft-ly of the dew-drops, Car-ol of the sun-shine too,
3. War-ble sweet-ly of the dawn-ing, Car-ol of the noon-tide hour,
4. Bon-nie warblers, mer-ry warblers, Sweet your mel-o-dy to me,

Chant to me your sweetest car-ol, Mute-ly I will lis-ten now.
Mak-ing bright these golden hours, Sing of sun-ny skies so blue.
Sing a ten-der song of sun-set, War-ble of your leaf-y bower.
Mer-ry song-sters, I would greet you, Car-ol sweet-ly, blithe, and free.

CHORUS.

Mer-ry, mer-ry warblers, trill your lay, Let your car-ols ring,

Sway-ing in the branches all the day, Bon-nie birds of spring,

Merry Warblers.—Concluded.

Hap-py lit-tle songsters, light and free, Nev-er knew a care,

War-ble now your tune-ful songs to me, Bon-nie birds of air.

No. 4. GOOD MORNING.

Lizzie A. Switzer. G. W. Fields.

1. Good morn-ing, now, dear teach-er, And schoolmates ev-'ry one,
2. Good morn-ing, now, to les-sons, We'll try to learn you well,
3. Good morn-ing, dear old playground, We hail thee with our might,
4. So, now, to all, Good morn-ing, Make this a hap-py day,

May pleas-ure be a fea-ture Of work from sun to sun;
And not mis-count our bless-ing. As man-y we've heard tell,
No place is there to be found Af-ford-ing more de-light.
Mind teach-er's ev-'ry warn-ing, And walk in wis-dom's way.

Cres.

Good Morning.—Concluded.

We think a hap-py greet-ing Will help our work all day,
Who spent their time in play-ing, Which sad - ly they re - pent;
O mer - ry games for play-ing, We'll try your mag - ic spell,
In man-hood, when we're rul - ing Our coun-try large and grand,

While swift the hours are fleet-ing, Filled up with work or play.
But no a - mount of pray-ing A - tones for time mis - spent.
But know that not by weigh-ing Can an - y your wealth tell.
Then may we by our school-ing Help bless our no - ble land.

CHORUS.

Good morn-ing, one, Good morn-ing, all, Our hearts are light and free,

Then cheer-ful-ly and mer - ri - ly We sing our greet-ing glee.

No. 5.   THOSE EVENING BELLS.

Thos. Moore.   J. F. King.

Moderate.

1. Those evening bells! . . . those evening bells! . . .
2. Those joy-ous hours . . . are passed a - way, . . .
3. And so 'twill be . . . when I am gone, . . .

How many a tale . . . . their mu-sic tells, . . .
And many a heart . . . . that then was gay, . . .
That tune - ful peal . . . . will still ring on, . . .

Of youth and home . . . and that sweet time, . . .
Within the tomb . . . now dark - ly dwells, . . .
While oth-er bards . . . shall walk these dells, . . .

NOTE. These beautiful lines were suggested to the author, by the following incident: A chime of bells were cast in Italy by one who enjoyed their sweet music very much. By some resolution the bells were taken away and the maker became an exile. After many years he wandered to Ireland, where his trained ear suddenly caught the sweet sound of his bells, as it floated on the calm evening air, and with it came the hallowed associations and scenes of his early life. As he listened the tide of memories that came vibrating through his heart snapped its strings and his spirit fled.

Those Evening Bells.—Concluded.

When last I heard . . their soothing chime. (their soothing chime.)
And hears no more . . those evening bells. (those evening bells.)
And sing your praise, . . sweet evening bells. (sweet evening bells.)

REFRAIN. A tempo.

Those evening bells, those evening bells, How many a

tale, their music tells, Of youth and home, And that sweet

time, When last I heard their soothing chime.

No. 6.

OUR NATION.

LAURA E. NEWELL.

E. A. GLENN.

With Energy.

f

1. Our glo-rious land............ to all so dear,........ The
2. When shadowed by .... war's cru-el din,...... ... When
3. Co-lum-bia, thou.. .... shalt ev-er shine,........ As

m *p*

pride of ev - - 'ry heart sin-cere, ... Is
clam-or reigned .... with-out, with-in, ... Thy
gem en-shrined, ... What pow'r is thine, ... A

f

now and ev - - er-more shall be .... The
no-ble sons .... un-daunt-ed fell, ... De-
might-y na - - tion, all re-joice .... In

3

ff

CHORUS.

home of peace and lib-er - ty.
fend - ing homes they loved so well.
lib - er - ty with heart and voice.

3

f

A - mer - i-

A - mer - i - ca, O sun - ny land,

a, ... O sun - ny land, ... Thy

Thy sons re - joice,

sons re - joice, ... A loy - al

A loy - al band ev - er shall be.

band, ... As now thou ev - er - more shalt

The gem of all na - tions great and free.

be, ... The gem of na - tions, great and free.

SCIENCE HILL.

Lizzie A. Switzer.

G. W. Fields.

1. We will climb the hill of science, We will walk in wisdom's way,
2. We will la-bor with-out ceasing, We will nev-er stop to sigh,

We will ev-'ry day be learn-ing, We will hast-en on our way.
Far-ther still our view in-creas-ing, We have set our mot-to high,

Ev-'ry day our path-way brightens, Beauties ev-'ry-where ap pear,
Those who la-bor win the lau-rels, We will la-bor with our might.

Will-ing minds our la-bor light-en, And suc-ceed-ing bring good cheer.
We will climb the hill of sci-ence, We will reach the top-most height.

Science Hill.—Concluded.

No. 8. THE MERRY BELLS OF CHRISTMAS.

8. 8. T.

S. S. TURLEY.

Spirited.

1. The mer-ry bells of Christmas, Ring out the gold-en chime, And
2. The mer-ry bells of Christmas, Toll on with joy-ful sound, And
3. The mer-ry bells of Christmas, Chime on with glad re-frain, The

tell to ev-'ry na-tion, Of ev-'ry land and clime, Go
may the love of Je-sus, In ev-'ry heart a-bound, Go
love of our dear Sav-iour, O bless-ed be His name, He

tell the old, old sto-ry, Of Christ, our Lord and King, 'Tis
tell to ev-'ry na-tion, The song of Je-sus' birth, And
came on earth to save us, And give His bless-ed Word, It

peace on earth, good will to men, Glad hal-le-lu-jahs sing.
let the peo-ple shout a-loud, With glad and joy-ful mirth.
bids us come to Je-sus, The pre-cious, Ho-ly Lord.

The Merry Bells of Christmas.—Concluded.

CHORUS.

Then glo - ry, hal - le - lu - jah! Then glo - ry, hal - le - lu - jah! Then

glo - ry, hal - le - lu - jah! We are com-ing, Lord of all. Then

glo - ry, hal - le - lu - jah! Then glo - ry, hal - le - lu - jah! Then

glo - ry hal - le - lu - jah! We are com - ing at His call.

No. 9. CHILDREN'S DAY.

Maggie E. Gregory.   Chas. H. Gabriel.

Primary Department.

1. O hap - py, sun - ny month of June, Of sing - ing birds and
2. While hap - py birds their tune - ful songs Are pour - ing forth un-
3. The same kind Sav - iour who on earth Said "Suf - fer lit - tle

fra - grant flow'rs, When we can greet the Children's Day, And
to their King, Let us u - nite with one ac - cord, His
ones to come," Will hear our praise, ac - cept our love, And

Intermediate Department.

Cres.   f

meet to spend its hap - py hours. Up - on the glad-some
love to tell, His praise to sing. As flow - ers in their
guide us to our heaven-ly home. There in that land of

m

Chil-dren's Day, The day we love so well, Our songs of praise and
beau - ty bloom, Their fragrance shed a - part, So let us to our
pure de - light All tears are wiped a - way; There we shall meet to

Children's Day.—Concluded.

words of prayer, Our thanks to Christ shall tell.
Sav-iour bring Sweet in-cense from the heart.
part no more, Thro' our glad Children's Day.

With - in our
With - in our Fa-ther's

Fa - ther's house we meet In His dear
house we meet In His dear name. up - on His day, We'll plead His lit - tle

name, up - on His day, We'll
ones to join When-e'er we meet to praise and pray.

plead His lit tle ones to join Pc vn u.y o se and pray.

No. 10. OLD GLORY.

LAURA E. NEWELL. (*Rhythm "Yankee Doodle."*) J. F. KING.

1. There is a flag, a na - tions flag,—Which tells a
2. In time of peace, or time of war, The stars and
3. Three cheers! the red, the white, the blue, Our flag a -

D. C.—is a flag, a na - tion's flag, Which tells a

death-less sto - ry, Both far and near it doth ap-
stripes we'll cher - ish, No ty - rant hands one fold shall
loft for - ev - er! We love the em - blem of the
death-less sto - ry, Both far and near it doth ap-

Omit after D. C. and go to Chorus.

pear, The flag that's called "Old Glo - ry." It floats on
mar, Who would, must sure - ly per - ish. Our em - blem
true, No pow'r this love shall sev - er. The cher - ished
pear. The flag that's called "Old Glo - ry."

land and on the sea, A - bove the roll - ing
blest we will pro - tect, Our Na - tion's sons de-
flag of Wash - ing - ton, A Na - tion's pride re-

Old Glory.—Concluded.

wa - ters, 'Tis loved by all, both great and small, Co-
fend it, No foe can rise to seize our prize, Or
main - ing, Is held more dear each com - ing year, New

D. C. then Chorus.   **CHORUS.**

lum - bia's sons and daugh - ters.   Don't you hear from
dare to mad - ly rend it.
lau - rels still 'tis gain - ing.
D. C.—There

east and west, The ev - er thrill - ing sto - ry: Of

this our flag, the fair - est, best? Our Na - tion's dear "Old Glo - ry!"

No. 11. YOUTHFUL FRIENDS.

Lizzie A. Switzer.

G. W. Fields.

Not too slow.

1. Hap-py fac-es we hold dear, In the school-room do ap-pear,
2. Learn-ing ear-ly in bright youth, Wisdom's ways are ways of truth,
3. Youthful friendships, O how sweet, Life with-out is in-com-plete,
4. Love-ly spring-time, bringing cheer, Hap-piest sea-son of the year,

Wear-ing sun-shine with a grace, Which no artist's brush can trace.
Build-ing char-ac-ters of worth, Grandest structures found on earth.
Love-ly pic-tures, dear to all, Ear-ly hung on mem'ry's wall.
Youth-ful days, O may you bring, Win-ter age, bright pearls to string.

CHORUS.

Vis - ions back - ward, pleas - ure lends,
Vis-ions backward, pleasure lends, Vis-ions backward, pleasure lends,

Sweet - est thoughts of youth - ful friends.
Sweetest thoughts of youthful friends, Sweetest thoughts of youthful friends.

Repeat pp.

No. 12. A SONG FOR SUMMER TIME.

MARY D. BRINE.
Moderato.

WM. BEERY.

1. Sing a song for sum-mer-time, Hap-py, mer-ry days!
2. Noth-ing in the mead-ow grows— Be it e'er so wide—
3. Ev - 'ry lit - tle run-ning brook, Ev - 'ry lake and sea,
4. Hap - py, mer - ry sum-mer-time! How it loves to show

When all na - ture seems to be Run - ning o'er with praise;
Which can - not our ev - 'ry thought To the dear Lord guide.
Sings, and tells the love of God Giv - en us so free.
All the dear Lord's gifts to man On this earth be - low!

To the Giv - er of all good, All things fair and light,
Noth - ing blos - soms, noth - ing blooms, Be it large or small,
Sun and shad - ow in the sky Come they as they may,
With the sum - mer birds we sing Will - ing songs of praise.

All things beau - ti - ful, that make Liv - ing a de - light.
Which does not the glo - ry give To the Lord of all.
Yet but teach the lov - ing care Of our Lord each day.
May our hearts for Je - sus grow With the sum - mer days.

No. 13. THE JOLLY FARMER'S GIRL.

P. L. WARREN.

C. A. FYKE.

Lively.

1. Oh, I'm a jol - ly farm - er's girl, And a farm - er's wife I'll
2. Give me a hap - py farm - er's home, Far a - way from the cit - y's

be, No dap - per clerk with a mus - tache twirl, Or
din, So sweet - ly pure and so no - bly true, Temp-

cit - y dude for me, ha! ha! For the sweet-est home and the
ta - tion can't come in, ha! ha! For the tru - est love and the

sweet-est flowers and the sweet-est qui - et life, The short - est days
tru - est friends, and the tru - est wed-ded life, The sweet- est dreams

The Jolly Farmer's Girl. —Concluded.

and the hap - pi - est hours, Be - long to the farm-er's wife.
and the bright-est joys, Be - long to the farm-er's wife

Whistling Chorus.

THE VALLEY OF BLESSING.

MRS. A. P. JARVIS.

N. W. KIRE.

Not too fast.

1. I know of a beau-ti-ful val-ley In which I would wan-der for aye;
2. In that beau-ti-ful val-ley of blessing With darkness we ne'er shall be cursed,
3. Oh! the beau-ti-ful val-ley of blessing, Where God's will is full and complete;

The smile God's love is up-on it, His presence sheds rapturous day.
For in all of brightness and glo-ry The sun in His fullness will burst.
Where we bow in true con-se-cra-tion, And lay all our lives at His feet.

This vale is the val-ley of bless-ing; Who enters may therein a-bide,
For He is the light and life-giv-ing; Ac-cept-ed in Him we shall stand,
May we live in the sunshine for-ev-er, Be-yond all our doubts and our fears,

And taste of the springs of God's mercy That well up on ev-er-y side.
Sur-ren-dered full to His keep-ing, And held by His gracious right hand.
Com-plete in glo-ri-ous like-ness, He'll wipe a-way all of our tears.

No. 15. HARVEST HOME.

REV. WM. APPEL.

CHAS. H. GABRIEL.

1. Oh, Thou source of ev-'ry bless-ing, Un-told rich-es still pos-
2. All our work and all our sow-ing, We have done in hope, well
3. Thou hast crowned the year with good-ness, And the countless sheaves bear

sess-ing, Giv-ing sun-shine, dew and rain, And the sheaves of ripened grain.
know-ing That our la-bor is in vain, Lest Thou givest sun and rain.
wit-ness Of a Father's care and love, And a boundless store a-bove.

CHORUS.

Har-vest home, ... har-vest home, We re-
Har-vest home, har-vest home,

joice in Thy great good-ness, For a plen-teous har-vest home,

Harvest Home.—Concluded.

Har - vest home, ... har - vest home, We re-
Har - vest home, har - vest home,

joice in Thy great good - ness, For a plen-teous har - vest home.

No. 16. THE BETHLEHEM BABE.

Words and Music by T. B. WEAVER.

1. Once in a low - ly man - ger, Hundreds of years a - go,
2. Jo - seph and Ma - ry, wea - ry, No one would take them in,
3. Far from the East, three strangers, Led by a star their way,

A lit - tle babe, so ho - ly, Came to this world be - low,
Slept in a sta - ble drear - y, Nigh to a crowd - ed inn.
Kept safe-ly from great dan - gers, Seek-ing the Christ, they say,

The Bethlehem Babe.—Concluded.

Near was a crowd-ed cit - y, Beth-le-hem, dark and old;
Out on the hill-side, frightened, Shepherds be-held a sight;
Came to the man-ger low - ly, Bringing their gifts of love;

Here Jo-seph sought for pit - y; Chill was the night and cold.
For all the sky was lightened On that De-cem-ber night.
Worshiped the babe so ho - ly, Gift of the world a - bove.

CHORUS.

1. and 2.– An-gels sang out the sweet sto - ry, "Fear not, for lo! this morn,
3 –Glo-ry to God in the high-est! Peace and good will to men!

Je-sus, the Christ of glo - ry, A lit-tle babe is born."
Glo-ry to God in the high-est! Ev - er A - men! A - men!

By per.

MARCHING ON.

LAURA E. NEWELL.

J. F. KING.

Moderato.

1. March-ing on - ward, all to - geth - er, Keep-ing step so
2. March-ing on - ward, on - ward ev - er, E'en tho' for - tune
3. March-ing on - ward, swell the cho - rus, Faith-ful sol - diers,

firm and true; March-ing on in sun - ny weath - er, Or 'neath
smile or frown; Naught from truth our hearts shall sev - er, Tho' we
one and all; God in love is smil - ing o'er us, On His

skies of la - den hue; March-ing on - ward, nev - er daunt - ed,
may not win re - nown; Still ad - vanc - ing, staunch and fear-less,
name for strength we call; On - ward till the stars of heav - en

With a heart and pur-pose strong, For the right shall tri-umph o-
On-ward, shall our mot - to be, On in might for truth and lib-
Gleam in evening's az - ure sky; On - ward marching, yes, we're march-

Marching On.—Concluded.

March-ing on,   March-ing

ver   wrong.
er - ty.
ing   on.

Marching, marching on.

on,

Yes, we're march-ing on, We're all marching, march-ing on, yes,

on,

march-ing, march-ing on,

March-ing on - ward, nev - er daunt - ed,
Still ad - vanc - ing, staunch and fear-less,
On - ward till the stars of heav - en

With a heart and purpose strong; For the right shall triumph o - ver wrong.
On-ward shall our mot - to be, On in might for truth and lib-er - ty.
Gleam in evening's a- zure sky : Onward shout for home and vic-to- ry !

No. 18. MORNING SONG.

T. B. WEAVER, By per.

With Energy.

1. Wel-come all to school this morning, Beau-ti - ful morn-ing! Beau-ti - ful
2. How our books so new we treasure, Beau-ti - ful les-sons! Beau-ti - ful
3. We shall nev - er once be tar - dy, Ev - er - y morn-ing, Ev - er - y
4. Lit - tle children have their sor - row, Beau-ti - ful childhood! Beau-ti - ful

morn-ing! To the school-bell's music ringing, All of our hearts are sing-ing.
les-sons! We shall stud-y them with pleasure, Try-ing to do our du - ty.
morn-ing. Stormy weather makes us hardy, Well as the golden sun-shine.
childhood! But for-get it on the mor-row, Beau-ti-ful, hap-py child-hood!

Here a - gain in friend-ly greet-ing, In our pleas-ant plac - es;
Books and tab - lets, pen - cils, pa - per, Desks, we'll keep so neat - ly;
In our school and in our class- es, We shall help each oth - er;
Words of wis - dom kind-ly spo - ken, By our friends that love us,

Teach-er, pu - pils in this meet - ing, See on - ly smil - ing fac - es.
And we'll try to do no ca - per, On - ly to mind com-plete - ly.
Do - ing what is right for pass - es, Just as a sis - ter, broth- er.
Heal our lit - tle hearts, tho' bro-ken, Pointing to God a - bove us.

No. 19. WHERE AUTUMN LEAVES GLOW.

Lizzie A. Switzer.　　　　　　　　　　　　　　　　　　G. W. Fields.

Gaily.

1. We will go with cheer, to the woodland near, Where the autumn leaves do glow,
2. We will gather leaves, while the soft wind grieves, While the soft winds gently blow.
3. To the home add cheer from the beauties here, By entwining garlands fair,

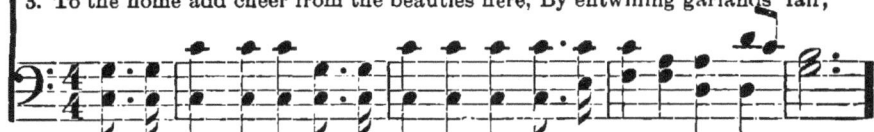

By the cold frost kissed and all wet with mist, They are falling sure and slow.
While our hopes are bright and our hearts are light, To the woods away we go.
Then in winter drear they will bring good cheer, As they lend their beauty rare.

CHORUS.

Autumn leaves, Au-tumn leaves, Where the autumn leaves do glow,
Autumn leaves, Autumn leaves,

Repeat pp.

Autumn leaves, Autumn leaves, To the woods a-way we go.
Autumn leaves, Autumn leaves,

By per.

No. 20. BEAUTIFUL FLOWERS.

R. S. H.

R. S. HANNA.

1. How dear to my heart are the beau-ti-ful flow'rs,
2. Thou wouldst still be a-dored as each mo-ment thou art,
3. Then gath-er the beau-ti-ful flow-ers of spring,

Which I gaze on so fond-ly to-day;
Let thy love-li-ness fade as it will;
And twine them in gar-lands so fair,

They bring re-col-lec-tions of loved ones at home,
For a-round ev-'ry blos-som each wish of my heart
I can nev-er for-get them, tho' far, far from home,

That will fol-low wher-ev-er I stray.
Would en-twine it-self ver-dant-ly still.
And time will but make them more dear.

Beautiful Flowers.—Concluded.

CHORUS.

p

Beau - - - ti - ful flow'rs, ...

Beau - ti - ful flow'rs,   Beau - ti - ful flow'rs,

m

Beau - - - ti - ful flow'rs, ...

Beau - ti - ful flow'rs,   Beau - ti - ful flow'rs,

f

Beau - - - ti - ful flow - - ers,

Beau - ti - ful flow'rs,   Beau - ti - ful flow'rs,

Dim.

For the beau - ti - ful chil - dren to wear.

DUTY.

H. M.

Harold Marlow.

Allegretto.

1. We are hap-py, ev-er hap-py when the day is
2. Yes, the du-ty that is near-est is the first to

new, As we meet and greet each oth-er with a
do; It will help us do the du-ty that will

love that's true; But a-round us we wiii find Work for
fol-low, too; And with all our du-ties done, As they

both the heart and mind, For the du-ty that is
come to ev-'ry one, We will high-er and still

Duty.—Concluded.

near - est   is   the   du - ty   we   must   do.
high - er   rise   to   per - fect   life   and   true.

CHORUS.

p   *m*   *cres.*

'Tis   the   du - ty   that   is   near - est,   Yes,   the

f   *p*

du - ty   we   must   do;   We   will   ev - er,

m   *f*

by   en - deav - or,   Do   each   du - ty   well   and   true.

By permission of author. Arranged by F. W. W.

No. 22.   MARCHING SONG.

Lulu Dilley

A. G Slife.

In march time.

1. We turn (1) at sig - nal num-ber one, At two (2) we're proudly standing,
2. For-ward (4) we're marching to and fro, Like soldiers brave we're speeding,
3. Our hands (5) a-bove our heads we clasp, To form (6) an arch they're meeting,
4. Now halt (9) the sig - nal came at last, 'Tis march-ing time no long - er,

Mark time, (3) now right, now left, you see, Our teacher dear com-mand-ing.
Al-though the school-book is the foe, To knowl-edge it is lead - ing.
And as we drop (7) them to our sides, A bow (8) we give in greet-ing.
Our ex - er - cis - es we will give, They make our muscles strong-er.

CHORUS.

Left, right, left, right, keep-ing time just so, On - ward, on - ward,

proud - ly we will go, Left, right, left, right, keep - ing

Explanatory.—Pupils all seated. At signal (1), turn. At (2), stand, with left foot forward. At (3), mark time; pupils should continue to mark time while singing chorus the first time. (4), March ; be careful about stepping to the music. (5), Clap hands above head. (6), Form arch above heads. (7), Drop hands to side. (8), Bow; this should be in unison. (9), At signal, children stop at their seats. (10), Ex-ercises should be given during the singing of the chorus.

Marching Song.—Concluded.

time just so, On - ward, on - ward, proud-ly we will go.

No. 23. TRY, TRY AGAIN.

J. F. KING.

1. 'Tis a les-son you should heed, Try, try a - gain; If at first you
2. Once or twice tho' you should fail, Try, try a - gain; If you would at
3. If you find your task is hard, Try, try a - gain; Time will bring you

don't succeed, Try, try a - gain; Then your courage should appear, For if
last prevail. Try, try a - gain; If we strive, 'tis no disgrace, Tho' we
your reward, Try, try a - gain; All that oth-er folks can do, Why, with

you will per - se - vere, You will conquer, nev - er fear; Try, try a - gain.
do not win the race, What should you do in the case? Try, try a - gain.
patience, should not you? On-ly keep this rule in view: Try, try a - gain.

NATIVE LAND.

T. B. W

Not too fast.

T. B. Weaver.

1. My Native Land, I love thee so, In all the earth, where'er I go,
2. My Native Land, for-ev-er shine! The hand that formed thee is di-vine,
3. My Native Land, thy mission fill, Thou art the song of "peace, good-will,"
4. My Native Land, may freedom's song, Thro'out thy coasts in chorus strong

Cres. *f* *m*

No skies to me so blue as thine, No stars so bright as 'bove thee shine
To all the world thou art the star, That holds the gaze of all a - far.
Put not thy trust in war's affright, But in thy God, thy sons and right.
For-ev - er stir our love for thee, Thou land of peace and lib - er - ty.

CHORUS.

f *m* *Cres.*

I love thy flag, my na-tive sign, I love it as this life of mine;

mf *cres.* *f*

Its folds of red and white and blue, Were saved by men, so brave and so true.

By permission of author.

No. 25. THE BIRDIES' SONG.

Lulu Dilley Donica. T. B. Weaver.

Solo.

1. Tweet! Tweet! Tweet! Tweet! On the branch-es high
2. Tweet! Tweet! Tweet! Tweet! Climb up there and see
3. Tweet! Tweet! Tweet! Tweet! Do not harm them, pray;
4. Tweet! Tweet! Tweet! Tweet! When the nights grow long,

Sits the rob - in red - breast, Sing - ing mer - ri - ly;
Why he is so hap - py, Sing - ing glad and free;
He will be so cheer - ful, If you'll let them stay:
When the wind comes howl - ing, He will cease his song;

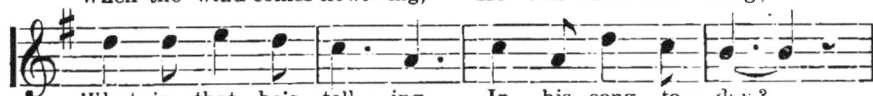

What is that he's tell - ing In his song to - day?
Mam - ma bird is hid - ing Un - der - neath her breast,
In the mer - ry sun - shine, All the sum - mer long,
To the south he'll hast - en, With his bird - ies dear,

List - en, and you'll hear him, This is what he'll say:
Three such lit - tle bird - ies Snug - ly in the nest-
He will then be sing - ing, This will be his song:
If you list - en close - ly, These glad words you'll hear:

CHORUS. f

Tweet! Tweet! Tweet! Tweet! Lit - tle girls and boys!

Cres. f

Tweet! Tweet! Tweet! Tweet! Tweet! Life is full of joys!

THE WATERMILL.

A. K. Mills.
G. W. Fields.

Playfully.

1. When spring-time comes with fair - y - step Up - on the sun-
2. It calls us back to hap - py days, When 'neath a cloud-
3. Thus ev - er like the run-ning stream, Our days glide swift-

ny hill, We love to wan - der by the stream, And
less sky, We wandered to the wa - ter - mill To
ly a - way, And tho' they bring us joy or grief, They

lis - ten to the mill. We think, as there we stand a - lone,
watch the stream go by. Oh, hap - py days, we loved so well,
nev - er come to stay. They turn a - while the old mill - wheel,

As the brook-let murmurs past, That the mill will nev - er
They could not al - ways last, But like the wa - ter
To grind the gold - en grain, Then like the wa - ter

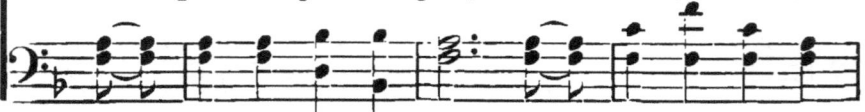

The Watermill.—Concluded.

grind a - gain With the wa - ter that has passed.
by the mill, They glid - ed on too fast.
in the brook, They nev - er come a - gain.

CHORUS.

Then list - en to the wa - ter - mill, (wa - ter - mill,) As the

brook - let mur - murs by, ... Oh, the mill will nev-

er grind a - gain With the wa - ter that has passed.

No. 27. WHEN THE CHILDREN ARE GROWN.

E. R. LATTA.   FRANK M. DAVIS.

1. When the chil - dren are small, And de - pend on our care,
2. When the chil - dren are small, And are mer - ry at play,
3. When the chil - dren are small, We may guide them at will;

Though our task may be hard, Our pro - tec - tion they share;
We look on with a smile, And as hap - py as they;
But when old - er they grow, They may stray in - to ill;

And 'tis bet - ter, by far, Than is dwell - ing a - lone,
But we think with a pang, Of each ges - ture and tone,
They may nev - er a - gain Be so ful - ly our own:

In the home - stead, so still, When the chil - dren are grown.
When the days are long past, And the chil - dren are grown.
But our love lin - gers yet, When the chil - dren are grown.

When the Children are Grown.—Concluded.

When the chil - - dren are grown,
When the chil - dren are grown, When the chil - dren are grown,

And are bid - ding a - loof From the shel - ter - ing roof,

They are ev - - er our own,
They are ev - er our own, They are ev - er our own,

And our love is not lost, When the chil - dren are grown.

WELCOME HOME.

Harold Marlow.

Moderato

p   *m*

1. Wel - come home (welcome home), wel - come home (welcome home),
2. We have missed (we have missed), we have missed (we have missed),
3. God pro - tect (God pro - tect), God pro - tect (God pro - tect),

f

Wel - come home   to those who love you   well (love you well);
We have missed   you while you were a - way (were a - way);
God pro - tect   and give His peace to   you (peace to you);

p   *m*

Heart and hand (heart and hand), heart and hand (heart and hand),
Your re - turn (your re - turn), your re - turn (your re - turn),
Be your Guide (be your Guide), be your Guide (be your Guide),

f

Heart and hand will join their joy to tell.
Your re - turn brings joy to all to - day.
Be your Guide in all that you may do.

By permission of author.

Welcome Home.—Concluded.

Yes, we wel - come, we welcome you home a - gain, With

hearts o'er - joyed we meet, And hands out-stretched we greet;

Yes, we wel - come, we welcome you home a - gain: What-

e'er be ours to do, We wel - come you!

No. 29. SWEET SUMMER'S GONE AWAY.

J. V. KING.

Moderato.

1. There's a pur - ple tint on the wood - land leaves,
2. In the wrin - kled brook no ros - es peep,
3. On the brow - ing field the spi - der spins.
4. There are lov - ing arms for the ba - by dear,

And the winds are up all day; There's a
And the bees no long - er stay; And the
Where the lambs no long - er play; And the
Though the skies are chill and gray; And a

rust - ling heard in the yel - low sheaves, And it
but - ter - flies have gone to sleep, And the
crick - et now his chirp be - gins, And the
co - zy home - nest all the year, And sweet

seems to sad - ly say: Sweet sum - mer,
lo - cust trills all day.
quail is whist - ling gay. Sweet sum - mer's gone a - way,
kiss - es ev - 'ry day.

CHORUS.

Sweet Summer's Gone Away.—Concluded.

Sweet sum - mer,
Sweet sum - mer's gone a - way, Sweet

sum - mer's gone a - way, gone a - way! Sweet
Sweet

sum - mer, Sweet sum - mer
sum - mer's gone a - way! Sweet sum-mer's gone a - way!

Rit. *Repeat pp.*

Sweet sum - mer's gone a - way! gone a - way!

MERRY MAY.

Lively.

J. F. KING.

1. Mer - ry May comes lightly trip-ping 'Thro' the woods and meadows gay,
2. Now the blue-eyed heaven's glanc-es Brightly on the wa - ters play,

O'er the grass - y car - pet skip-ping, Welcome, welcome, mer - ry May.
Where the sil - ver bub-ble dan - ces, Welcome, welcome, mer -ry May.

CHORUS.

Mer - ry May, Mer - ry May, Mer -ry May, Mer - ry May, O mer - ry,

mer - ry, mer - ry, mer - ry May, mer-ry May, Mer-ry May, Mer -ry May,

Merry May.—Concluded.

Mer-ry May, Mer-ry May, O mer-ry, mer-ry, mer-ry, mer-ry May.

No. 31.   MORNING PRAYER.

LAURA E. NEWELL.

J. F. KING.

Andante.

1. Fa-ther in heav- en, hear us while we pray, Grant us Thy guidance
2. Thou hast been with us in the days gone by, Still be our por - tion,
3. Je - sus our Sav-iour, in life's coming days, Help us to serve Thee,

this coming day, Lead us in paths of peace, on in the
be ev - er nigh, All, all we trust to Thee, be Thou our
Thine be the praise, Still in the nar-row way, keep us Thine

light, Strengthen our pur - pose, that we live a - right.
stay, Shield us from dan - ger, all life's changeful way.
own, Till called to wor - ship Thee be - side Thy throne.

No. 32. THE MOCKING BIRD'S QUESTION.

FLORENCE N. REYNOLDS.

J. F. KROE.

Moderato.

1. In the or-ange tree in the dis-tance, I hear the mock ing
2. Dear lit-tle bird, should I an-swer? Do you think you could ev-

bird sing; O bright and sun-ny the weath-er, Now
er know The height of hu - man pleas-ure, The

in the ear-ly spring, His notes are clear and
depth of hu-man woe? Sing to your mate in the

mel-low, Mel-o-dious to the ear, He mer-ri-ly
tree-top, Your song so sweet and clear, But ask not your

The Mocking Bird's Question.—Concluded.

asks the ques - tion: "What cheer? what cheer? what cheer?"
mor - tal neigh - bor The ques - tion of "what cheer?"

REFRAIN.

Still ev - 'ry spring I hear it,— The notes to my heart

are dear; From or - ange, mag - no - lia, or

pine tree, The mock - ing bird's ques - tion, "what cheer."

No. 33. GOLDEN SUN OF EVENING.

Eva H. King.

Moderato.

1. Gold - en sun of eve - ning, In thy splen - did car,
2. Wel - come is thy beau - ty, Gold - en eve - ning sun,
3. Gold - en sun of eve - ning, We shall see no more,

To the west re - treat - ing, Rich thy glo - ries are.
Charm-ing is thy ra - diance, Just as day is done.
Till your light ap - proach - es From the east - ern shore.

Sun I love to view thee, Since I lisped thy name,
Thou must be ex - tinguished, Quenched each gold-en ray,
Then in morn - ing splen - dor, As you light the skies,

Since I learned thy glo - ries From Je - ho - vah came.
My im - mor - tal spir - it Can not fade a - way.
Call - ing us from slum - ber, Bid - ding us a - rise.

No. 34. SPRING - TIME.

Not too slow.

J. L. Sage.

1. { Oh, the mer-ry chime of the sweet spring-time, When the warm sun has melt-
   And the brooklets sing with a mer-ry ring, When their (OMIT............

2. { Now the children play o'er the grassy way, Hear their laugh and their shout
   And from feathered throats hear the sweetest notes, There is (OMIT..........

ed the snow:
.... i - cy fet-ters go.   Children, come
fill the air;
.... mu-sic ev-'ry - where.   Children come in the spring,

CHORUS. f

and sing,   Hear the mu - sic sweet and fair, Bring your
while song-birds sing,

flow-ers sweet, in wreaths so neat, Lovely fragrance will fill the air.
flow - ers neat,

HAPPY IN THE SUNLIGHT.

G. B. FIELDS.

Lively. _m_

1. Hap - py in the sun - light, Hap - py in the shad - ow,
2. Nev - er pain or sor - row Will we ev - er bor - row,
3. Mu - sic is a treas - ure, Use it with - out meas - ure;

Al - ways full of mu - sic bright and gay;
But we'll seek the good in ev - 'ry thing;
You will be the bet - ter for the same;

Roam - ing thro' the for - est, O'er the sun - ny mead - ow,
Cast - ing out the e - vil, Trust - ing in the mor - row,
It will make you joy - ful, And will give you pleas - ure,

Full of joy and rap - ture all the day.
For the sun - shine com - eth af - ter rain.
Drive a - way all weep - ing, ban - ish pain.

Happy In the Sunlight.—Concluded.

CHORUS.

Tra, la, la, la, la, la, la, la, la, la,

We are hap - py, light and gay, ...

Hap - py in the sun - light, Hap - py in the shad - ow,

Full of fun and mu - sic all the day. (all the day.)

No. 36.

MERRILY O!

Laura E. Newell.

J. F. King.

Lively. *m*

1. Mer - ri - ly trill the lay, Mu - sic is king to - day,
2. Beau - ti - ful days glide by, Swift - ly the mo - ments fly,

D. C.—Mer - ri - ly gay and free, Car - ol your songs of glee,

f

Joy - ful - ly sing, ... tune - ful - ly ring,
Si - lent - ly go, ... mer - ri - ly O,
Sun - ny the day, ... light zephyrs play,

m

Cheer - i - ly now pro - long, snatches of sil - v'ry song.
Ra - di - ant, glad, and bright, sea - sons of pure de - light,
Mur - mur - ing wa - ters flow, down where the lil - ies grow,

f Fine. *m*

Mer - ri - ly O! Mer - ri - ly O! Car - ol - ing
Mer - ri - ly O! Mer - ri - ly O! Blithely the
Mer - ri - ly O! Mer - ri - ly O!

Merrily O!—Concluded.

songs of love, Mirth-ful - ly on we rove, Buoy-ant our
wild - birds sing, Sweet-ly the ech - oes ring, Light-ly the

youth - ful hearts, buoy-ant and free, Mer - ri - ly
tones re - sound, sil - v'ry the sound, Soft - ly the

trill the lay, Mu - sic holds match - less sway,
glad re - frain Ech - oes a - gain, a - gain,

On - ward we'll gai - ly go, Mer - ri - ly O!
Soft - ly, and sweet, and low, Mer - ri - ly O!

No. 37.

GOLDEN MOMENTS.

LAURA E. NEWELL.

J. F. KING.

Syncopation.

Moderato.

1. The moments, the moments, So swift - ly they van-
2. The moments, the moments Are si - lent - ly fly-
3. The moments, the moments, So pre - cious and so fleet-

ish, No hand can ar - rest them, Nor hin - der their go-
ing, An hour lost can nev - er, No nev - er be o'er - tak-
ing, Then cher - ish them, prize them, The swift-winged and gold-

ing, All thoughts of wrong - do - ing Hearts sure -ly must ban-
en, We'll waste not these jew - els In dream-ing and sigh-
en, The years of our life are So swift - ly re - treat-

ish, And strive, ev - er strive, Good seed to still be sow - ing.
ing, But glean all these years, Let hearts to hope a - wak - en.
ing. Soon these sun - ny days Will be a time that's "old - en."

Golden Moments.—Concluded.

f

On - ward, school-mates! on - ward! Fear - less ev - er,

on - ward, school-mates! on - ward! Fal - ter nev - er!

On, with pur - pose true, And nought shall sev - er

Us from tread - ing hon - or's way!

No. 38. LIFE'S MORNING.

LAURA E. NEWELL.

J. F. KING.

1. There's a song in the air, and the skies are so fair, There's an absence of
2. While the dew's on the flow'rs all these glorious hours, All the air is with
3. In these glad days of youth, we will garner of truth, Rich supplies that will

care and strife, And our hearts are so light from the dawning till night, In the
fragrance rife, And our task we'll pursue, with a high aim in view, In the
use-ful be, In the years yet in store, when our school days are o'er, And this

D.S.—*Earth's a vis-ion so sweet, and its joys are complete, In the*

REFRAIN. *f*

beau - ti - ful morn-ing of life.
beau - ti - ful morn-ing of life.   We'll re-joice, we'll re-joice, We'll re-
scene but a sweet mem-o - ry.

beau - ti - ful morn-ing of life.

Cres.   *Rit. and Dim.*   **D. S.**

joice, we'll re-joice In the beau - ti - ful morn-ing of   life. (of life.)

BRIGHT MAY MORNING.

W. J. W.

WILL. J. WEAVER.

Lively.

1. There is joy in a bright May morning, That is sweet to the heart in the spring,
2. There is joy in a bright May morning, There are birds and the blossoms so fair,

When the birds are so sweetly out-pouring Their song, yes, their song sweetly sing.
When all na-ture is sweetly out-pouring Its songs, yes, its joy sweet and clear.

CHORUS.

O sweet May, blooming May, Now your praise we will sing;

La, la, la, la, la, la, la, la, la, la, la, la, la, la, la,

When the birds sweetly sing. *Observe hold and Rit. in repeat only.*
Rit.

La, la, la, la, la, la, la, Their song, yes, their song sweetly sing,
yes, sing.

MAYING WE WILL GO.

J. F. Kinne.

Cheerful.

1. Lo! the glad May morn With her ro - sy light is breaking O'er the
2. O'er the rus - tic wild Where the i - dle winds are blowing, We will
3. Oh! the glad May morn! Like a child she comes to meet us, With her

hill so love - ly and fair; And the pure young buds, From the dewy sleep a-
roam with pleasure to- day; On the mossy bank, Where the crystal brook is
brow all covered with flow'rs; And she calls the birds, All the merry birds, to

CHORUS.

Then a-way,

wak-ing, Mirth and music float in the air. Then a-way, a-way, a-way,
flowing, We will crown our queen of May.
greet us, And the laughing, bright summer hours.

Then a-way,

Then a - way, a - way, a - way, And a May - ing we will go!

MERRY SONG.

J. F. Kinг.

Gaily.

1. Join us in our mer - ry song, Tra la la la la, Tra la la la la,
2. Gent-ly now our voi - ces ring, Tra la la la la, Tra la la la la,

Swift to pass the hours a - long, Tra la la la la la la la.
Joy - ous as the birds of spring, Tra la la la la la la la.

Swing-ing, shout-ing as we go, Swing-ing gai - ly to and fro,
Not a thought of care have we, Hap - py, hap - py ev - er be.

Mak-ing life with pleas-ure glow, Tra la la la la la la.
Join us in our mer - ry glee, Tra la la la la la la.

No. 42.
G. W. F.

GOOD - NIGHT.

G. W. Fields.

1. Kind friends, we now come to the close, Our ev'nings work is done,
2. Good - night to all un - til a - gain We meet in splendor bright,

May you know naught but sweet re-pose, Good-night to ev - 'ry one.
May God be with you all till then, Good-night, kind friends, good-night.

CHORUS.

Good - night, good - night, Un - til the morn-ing light,
Good-night, good-night,

Good-night, good-night, good-night, good-night, Good-night, kind friends, good-night.

PART II

HAPPY GREETING.

LAURA E. NEWELL.

J. F. KING.

Gaily.

1. 'Tis with mer - ry hearts and voic - es That we bid you
2. Stead-fast bonds of friend-ship bind us, Links that ne'er shall
3. Oh! these moments, bright and gold - en, Spent in stud - y,

wel - come here, Hap - py greet - - ing! Hap - py
sev - ered be: Hap - py greet - - ing! Hap - py
still we'll prize! Hap - py greet - - ing! Hap - py

greet - - ing! Pray ac - cept this joy - ous trib - ute
greet - - ing! All these moments spent to - geth - er
greet - - ing! When life's sto - ry shall be old - en,

As a tok - en of our cheer; Welcome kind - ly, one and all.
Shall a - bide in mem - o - ry, As the past we oft re - call.
And shall gleam its sun-set skies, Mu - sic still shall hearts en - thrall.

Happy Greeting.—Concluded.

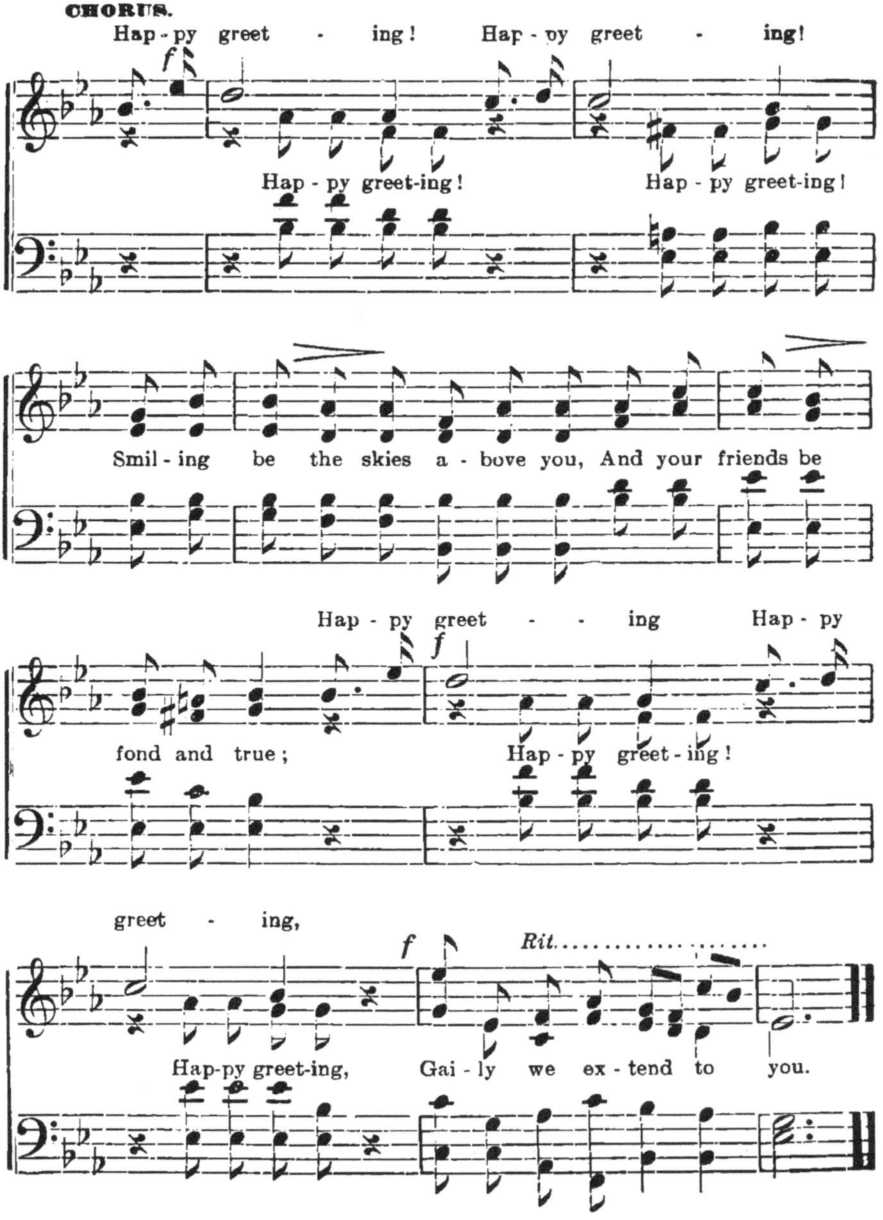

No. 2.   A MORNING SONG.

f. Eine.

1. A - wake from your slum - bers and come with a song,
2. The wood-lands are filled with sweet breath from the sky,
3. Leap o - ver the chasms with wings to your feet,

Thro' mead-ows and for - ests and wood - lands a - long;
Our steps is un - tir - ing our spir - its are high;
Climb up to the tree - tops, the heav - ens to greet.

The birds sing a wel - come the morn - ing and you,
The town at our backs and the moun-tains in view,
No oak of the for - est for us is too high,

And sip their first break - fast of new fall - en dew.
What joy is a - wait - ing your com - rades and you.
The far - ther from earth we are near - er the sky.

THE CRICKET.

Lively.

CHAUNCEY J. KING.

1. Lit - tle in-mate, full of mirth, Chirp-ing on my kitch-en hearth,
2. Thus thy praise shall be ex-pressed, In - of - fen - sive, wel-come guest!
3. Tho' in voice and shape they be, Formed as if a - kin to thee,

Where-so - e'er be thine a - bode, Al - ways har - bin - ger of good;
While the rat is on the scout, And the mouse with curious snout,
Thou sur-pass-eth, happier far, Hap-pi-est grasshoppers that they are;

Pay me for thy warm re - treat, With a song more soft and sweet,
With what verm-in else in - fest, Ev - 'ry dish, and spoil the best;
Theirs is but a sum - mer song, Thine en-dures the win - ter long,

In re-turn thou shalt re - ceive Such a strain as I can give.
Frisk-ing thus be - fore the fire, Thou hast all thy heart's de - sire.
Un-impaired, and shrill and clear, Mel - o - dy throughout the year.

A-DOWN THE DELL.

C. H. G.

Chas. H. Gabriel.

Moderato.

1. A-down the dell .... I love to roam, ... Where
2. A-down the dell............ I love to roam, ... To
3. A-down the dell............ I love to roam, ... When

fresh and sweet.......... the flow-ers bloom; .... Where
watch the shades........ of ev'-ning come; .... With
night has spread......... her cloak of gloom; .... For

birds of song, ... from bush and tree, ... Fill
phan-tom step............. they creep a - round, ... Yet
there I find............. a sweet re - lease,........ .... From

Cres.

Rit. and Dim.

all the air................. with mel - o - dy.................
ut - ter not .... a sin - gle sound............
ev - 'ry care, ... in per - fect peace. ....

A-Down the Dell.—Concluded.

A-down the dell . . . . I love to roam,

A-down the dell   I love to roam, With

With bird and bee, to make my home; . . . . My

bird and bee, ...   to make my home;

care and toil . . . . I leave be - hind,

My care and toil   I leave be-hind, And

And sweet con-tent-ment then I find.

sweet con - tent   -   ment then I find.

No. 5.

MERRY SONG.

J. M. DUNCAN.

1. Tra la la la, tra la la la, Tra la la la,
2. Tra la la la, tra la la la, Tra la la la,

tra la la la, Hear the children sing-ing, Hear the woodlands ringing,
tra la la la, Birds are gai-ly sing-ing, Their sweet tribute bringing,

Tra la la la, tra la la la, Tra la la la,
Tra la la la, tra la la la, Tra la la la,

tra la la la, Hear the feathered song-sters sing.
tra la la la, Hear the mer-ry chil-dren sing.

Merry Song.—Concluded.

Tra la la la, tra la la la, Tra la la la, tra la,

· Na - ture now re - joic - es, In their hap - py voic - es,

Tra la la la, Tra la la la la, Tra la la la,

Tra la, Hear them sing their mer - ry song.

No. 6. HOME IS WHERE THE HEART IS.

E. R. LATTA.

J. F KING.

Moderato.

1. Home is where the heart is, And where all a - gree;
2. Home is where the heart is, Tho' of wealth de - nied;
3. Home is where the heart is, Both by night and day;

Home is where the heart is, Hum - ble thou' it be,
Home is where the heart is, And the gen tle bide!
Home is where the heart is, And will ev - er stay!

Where each heart is faith - ful, And no e - vil harms;
Nei - ther pride nor fash - ion, There may find a place,
Where, in crowd-ed cit - y, Or the coun - try wide,

Cres. .... f

Love is more than splen - dor, More than beau-ty's charm!
But a look of kind - ness Shows on ev - 'ry face!
Lov - ing are the in - mates, What - so - e'er be - tide!

REFRAIN.

Home is where the heart is, And no frowns we see;

Home is where the heart is, Where-so-e'er it

Cres. . . . .

f *Rit. and Dim.* *m a tempo* *Cres.* . . . .

be; where'er it be; Where-so-e'er it be; Where-so-e'er it

f *p* *Cres.* *f* *Rit. and Dim.*

be; Home is where the heart is, Where-so-e'er it be.

THE MOUNTAINEER.

Laura E. Newell.

J. F. Kinsey.

Cheerful.

Tra la la, Tra la la,

1 Gai - ly sings the mountain-eer,   Tra la la,   Tra la la,
2. As he sings his mer - ry song,   Tra la la,   Tra la la,
3. Sturdy, fear - less as he sings,   Tra la la,   Tra la la,

Tra la la, Tra la la, FINE.

Ring his joy - ous notes so clear,   Tra la la,   Tra la la,
Ech-oes bear the tones a - long,   Tra la la,   Tra la la,
Joy is not con-fined to kings,   Tra la la,   Tra la la,

Brave his heart, his strength un-fail-ing, O'er the winding steeps he goes, Scal-ing
Na - ture's rare and radiant beauty, Gladdens all his onward way, While the
Son of Free-dom, loy - al ev - er To his country, God, and home, Light of

D.C.

now the rug - ged mountain, Pausing where a streamlet flows.
moun-tains in their grandeur, Add a glo - ry to the day.
heart, and strong of pur - pose, He with buoy - ant step doth roam.

WHIPPOORWILL.

Lula Dilley Donica.

J. H. Rosecrans.

1. Last night as the twi-light was fall - ing, The stars steal-ing
2. My dream-ing was o - ver that mo - ment, As I hastened to

out one by one, I wandered a - lone in the mead-ow,
aid the poor boy, Whose venturesome spir-it had led him In - to

Dreaming of days that were gone. And as I strolled on, sad-ly
do - ing some for - bid - den joy. But what do you think that I

mus - ing, A sound came from far o'er the hill,
no - ticed? The voice com - ing near - er still!

So plain - tive and clear came the ech - o,
And there in the bush - es I found him,

Of the voice call - ing, "Whip - poor - will!"
A bird, sing - ing "Whip - poor - will!"

Whippoorwill.—Concluded.

"Whip-poor-will, (poor Will!) Whip-poor-will, (poor Will!)" The

ech - o came back from the hill,

"Whip - poor - will, (poor Will!) Whip - poor - will,

(poor Will!)" "I won - der what's happened to Will!"

No. 9. WHISTLE AWAY, BOYS!

J. H. ROSECRANS.

1. Have you an - y pet - ty cares, boys? Then whistle them a - way;
2. 'Tis strange how soon friends gath-er A - bout a smil - ing face;

There's nothing cheers the spir - its Like mer - ry roun - de - lay.
That smil-ing eyes and lips count more Than beauty, wealth or grace.

No mat - ter for the heart-aches, 'Neath silk or sod - den gray,
But I have seen it tried, boys, When troubles come to stay,

For the sake of those who love you, Just whis-tle them a - way.
The brave heart leaps to work and strives To whis-tle it a - way.

Whistle Away, Boys!—Concluded.

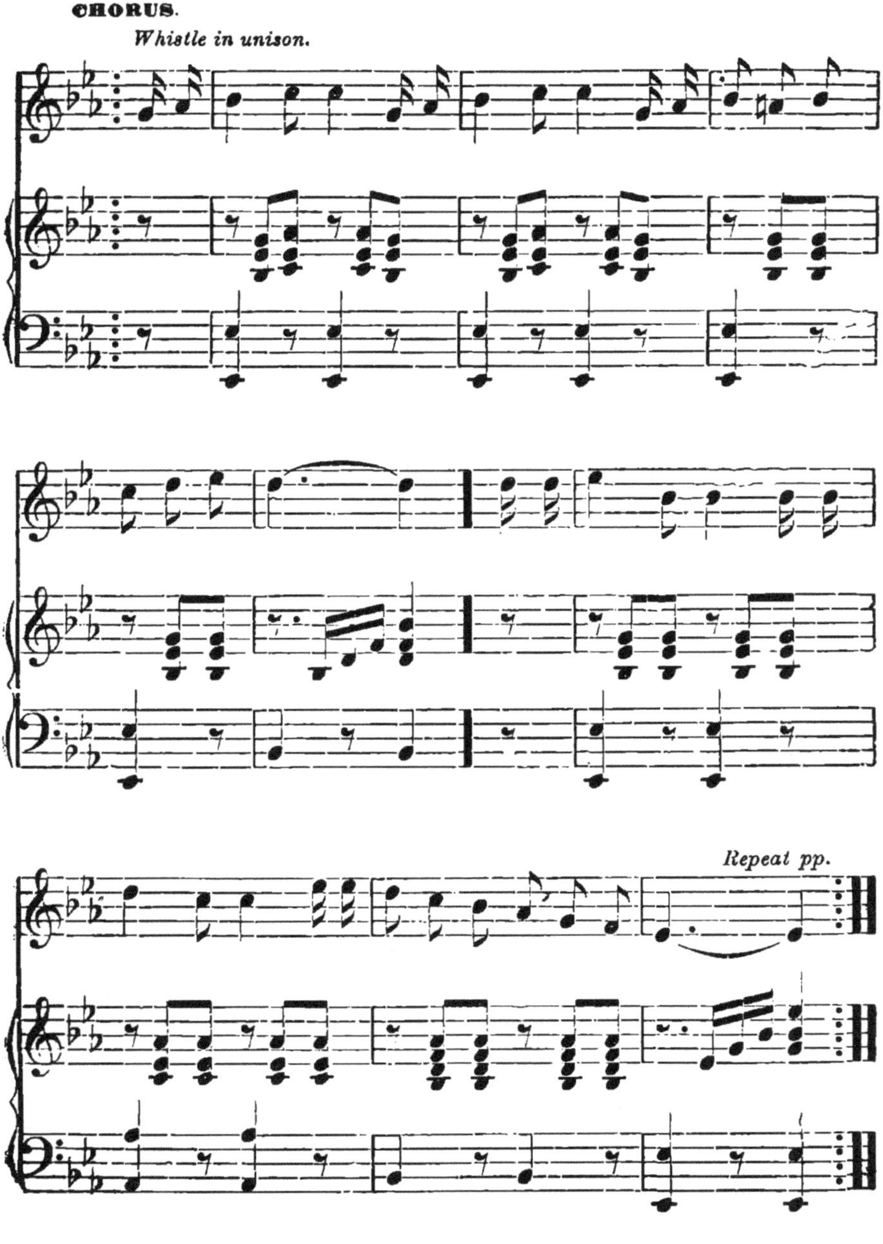

No. 10. THE RIVER'S SONG.

J. F. King.

Lightly

1. Far a - way, far a - way, In the sun - ny mead - ows,
2. Long a - go, long a - go, Sport - ed there sweet child - hood:
3. On - ward still, on - ward still, Is the riv - er glid - ing

Hear it now, hear it now, 'tis the riv - er's song;
Hear it now, hear it now, shout - ing o'er the wave,
To the sea, to the sea, like the stream of time:

Dip - ping, trip - ping, dash - ing, flashing, Thro' the mer - ry shad - ows,
Quaff - ing, laughing, sing - ing, springing, Thro' the tangled wild - wood,
Surg - ing, urg - ing, swell - ing, tell - ing, There is no de - lay - ing,

Cres......... ....f Dim...........

Beau - ti - ful and mus - i - cal it glides a - long.
O'er the rip - ple bend - ing, each young brow to lave.
Mur - mur - ing of o - cean, in a stream sub - lime.

SPRING SONG

Waltz movement.

Arr. by J. F. Kin.

1. Love - ly spring, O come thou hith - er, Spring be - loved, O
2. To the moun - tain would I hast - en, Rev - el in the
3. I would hear the shep - herd pi - ping, I would hear the

come a - gain; Bring us blos-soms, leaves and sing - ing, Deck a -
val - leys green; On the grass and flow'rs re - clin - ing, To en -
herd - bells ring; And re - joic - ing on the mead - ow, I would

gain the field and plain,
joy the sun - lit scene.
hear the sweet birds sing.

CHORUS.

La, la, la, la, la, la, la, la,
La, la,   la, la,

1

la, la, la, la, la, la, la, la.
la, la,   la, la.

2

la, la, la, la, la.
la, la, la.

No. 12.   BEAUTIFUL SUNSHINE.

G. B. F.

G. B. Fields.

Not too fast.

1. Oh, the sun-shine in my soul brings me near-er day by day,
2. Oh, the sun-shine in my soul drives my trou-ble all a-way.

To the bright and shin-ing goal so far a way; Where the
Makes me hap-py, light and free, yes, light and gay! And my

tree of life in bloom, in the world be-yond the tomb,
heart is filled with love, bathed in sun-shine from a-bove,

Sheds its fragrance to us on the rays of sun-shine
Filled with joy-ful tho'ts with hap-pi-ness and sun-shine.

Beautiful Sunshine.—Concluded.

Oh, the sun - - shine, beau-ti-ful sun - - shine,

Sun-shine in my soul, beau-ti-ful sun-shine in my soul,

Oh, the sun - - shine in my soul, ...

Sun-shine in my soul, the love-ly sun-shine in my soul,

Oh, the sun - - shine, beau-ti-ful sun - - shine,

Sun-shine in my soul, beau-ti-ful sun-shine in my soul,

Oh, the sun - shine in my soul.

Rit.

Oh, the sun - shine in my soul, (in my soul.)

No. 13.

ECHO SONG.

J. M. Duncan.

1. Gai-ly the mountaineer sings his song, Hil-e - i - o, Hil-e - i - o,
2. Light is the heart of the mountaineer, Hil-e - i - o, Hil-e - i - o,
3. Gladly his flocks hear his cheerful call, Hil-e - i - o, Hil-e - i - o,

List to the ech - o. so clear and strong, Mer-ri - ly bounding a - long.
Noth-ing he knows of dis-tress or fear, But is o'er-flowing with cheer.
Blithely it ech-oes from mountains tall, Floating in peace o - ver all.

CHORUS.

Hil-e - i - o, Hil-e - i - o, List to the song of the gay mountaineer,

Hil-e - i - o. Hil-e - i - o, List to his sweet song so clear.

MY MOUNTAIN HOME. J. P. KING.

Cheerful.

1. I love the wild hills of my mountain home, My mountain home, my
2. Oh, blue are the skies of my mountain home, My mountain home, my
3. I dream of thee of-ten, my mountain home, My mountain home, my

mountain home, Where, free as the breez-es, my foot-steps roam. My
mountain home, Where first the bright rays of the morn-ing come. The
mountain home, I'll love thee for-ev-er wher-e'er I roam, Wher-

CHORUS.

My home, my home,

bounding footsteps roam
rays of morning come.
e'er my footsteps roam.

My home, my home, my dearest home, my native mountain

home, my home, my home,

Rit. and Dim.

home, my home, my home, my home, my dearest home, My dear old mountain home.

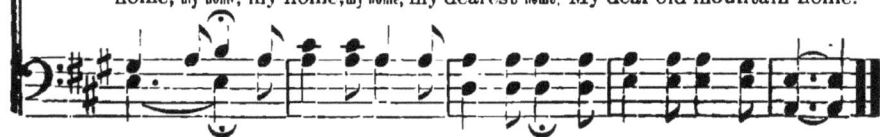

BIRD SONG.

W. A. CHRISTY.   J. F. KING.

Lightly. m

1. Swing-ing, swing-ing, hap-py and gay, In the leaf-y
2. In the ear-ly sum-mer's first dawn, When the win-ter's

for - est gray, Sweet - ly sings the wild - bird's song,
cold is gone, When the dew - y flow'rs ap - pear,

All the sum-mer day long; Care can ne'er dis-
Then his car-ols we hear, And when au-tumn,

Cres.

turb its dwell - ing, Nev - er bid its warb - ling cease,
cold and drear - y, Comes to hush his heed - less mirth,

Bird Song.—Concluded.

While with song his throat is swell-ing Na-ture's sweet-est
Sings he still as blithe and cheer-y, As when spring flow'rs

mel - o - dies.
deck the earth.

CHORUS.

Lit-tle bird, lit-tle bird, hap-py and free,

O were we on-ly as hap-py as thee! How would our singing o'er

val - ley and plain, An-swer the for-est re-frain

Repeat pp

No. 16. THE BIRDS CONCERT.

Laura E. Newell. J. F. King.

Waltz movement.

1. Oh, a blue-bird was mer - ri - ly sing - ing, On the limb of an
2. The blue-bird sang, "Winter is o - ver!" The rob-in chirped,
2. "The mar-tins are coming," quoth rob - in, "They'll tell us a

old ap-ple tree, When a rob-in came flitting close by him,
"Hap-py am I !" When stur-di - ly warbled the red - bird,
sto - ry, I know, Of what they have seen in their trav - els,

And a car - ol sang gai - ly with glee, When a red - bird ap-
"I stayed in the branches close by All win-ter while
They al - ways are read - y to go; And all of the

peared at the con - cert, And his voice loud-ly rang on the breeze,
some were mi - grat - ing; The *North* has no ter-rors for *me*."
rest of the rang - ers Will soon be a-mong us a - gain.

The Birds Concert.—Concluded.

When they all joined the mus - i - cal cho - rus, Till it rang thro' the
Then gai - ly they caroled to - geth - er, So blithe in the
But we are as hap - py as they are;" Then light - ly they

CHORUS.

old or-chard trees. Mer-ri-ly, cheer-i-ly, echoed the
old ap-ple tree
sang their re - frain.

song, Joy-ful-ly, glee-ful-ly tones they'd pro-long: There in the

boughs of the old ap-ple tree, Warbled these songsters in concert to me.

No. 17. SKATER'S SONG.

J. S. FEARIS.

1. A - way and a - way o'er the deep sounding tide, On crys-tals of sil-
2. Thro' pale mists of evening the sun glimmers still, And ling-ers a-while
3. Look up now! how sparkles the star-light-ed sky! And list to the mu-

ver we sweep and we glide, The steel is our pin - ion, our
on the brow of the hill; But now he's gone down, and with
sic as on - ward we fly, So joy - ful - ly, broth - er, we

roof the broad blue, And heav - en's pure breez - es our
soft tran - quil glow, The moon shines like sil - ver a-
float and we glide, In sun - light and moon - light, o'er

path - way pur - sue, Then a - way, then a - way, free and
bove and be - low, Then a - way, then a - way, free and
life's sil - ver tide, Then a - way, then a - way, free and

Skater's Song.—Concluded.

CHORUS.

Rit. *f Faster.*

gay. free and gay.　　Joy - ful - ly,　joy - ful - ly　on　we glide,

Mer - ri - ly　o - ver the　fro - zen tide, Speed-ing so cheer - i - ly

side　by　side, Sing-ing a　hap - py　song.　　Wak-ing the

ech - oes　on　ev - 'ry　side,　Mer - ri - ly　glid - ing　on.

PANSIES.

LAURA E. NEWELL.

R. A. GLENN.

1. Pansies, pansies, with your fa - ces bright, Glad your mis-sion,
2. Pansies, pansies, lis - ten now to me, Soft-ly, soft - ly,
3. Lightly, lightly, tripping o'er the lea, Soon, my pan-sies,
4. Pansies, pansies, "for a tho't," I know, This I'll whisper,

bringing heart's delight, Al-most speaking, "for a tho't," are you,
whisper I to thee, There's a maiden that I love full well,
will she come to me, Then a sto - ry I would fain re - peat:
that "I love her so." Pan-sies, pansies, lis - ten! do you hear?

Pansies fragrant, sparkling in the dew. Pansies, fair pansies, "for
That's my se-cret. pansies do not tell.
Low-ly kneeling at this maiden's feet.
She is coming! com-ing, she is near!

CHORUS.

tho't," are you, Beautiful blossoms 'neath skies of blue, Or 'neath the

Pansies.—Concluded.

frowns of a storm-y sky, Blos-som-ing bravely while clouds roll by.

No. 19. OVER THE SNOW.

Arr. by J. F. King.

Lively.

1. O - ver the val - ley of beautiful snow, Happy we go, Mer-ri-ly O!
2. List to the ringing and jingling of bells, Pleasure it tells, Louder it swells;
3. See with its bright lond the beautiful sleigh, Dashing away, Happy and gay;

Joy-ful all voi - ces as onward we glide, O-ver the glistening tide.
Mingling with songs of re-joic-ing and glee, From the glad spirits so free.
O-ver the snow in the cold freezing night, Moon-beams are glancing so bright.

Whistling Chorus.

No. 20.

GOD IS OUR GUIDE.

H. M.

Duet.

Harold Marlow.
Arr. by F. W. Westhoff.

Andante. *m*

1. In the si - lent hours of night, When the stars are shin - ing
2. In the si - lence, lis - ten well, Hear the mes - sage, it will

p

2. dark - ness com - eth light, ...
1. hear the voice of God.

bright, We can hear the voice, the voice of God, Whisp'ring
tell: Out of dark - ness com - eth, com - eth light, For the

Cres. *m*

thro' the sol - i - tude; Ev - 'ry mur - mur from a - far Seems a -
day must fol - low night, Hope as - cend - ing, is the dawn. Faith, tri -

p

2. heart is drawn a - bove...
1. breeze by which we're fan'd

kin to ev - 'ry star; Ev - 'ry breeze by which we are fan'd
um - phant, morn - ing sun; While each heart is drawn, is drawn a - bove

God Is Our Guide.—Concluded.

Seems a touch from His own hand. Oh, to feel that He is near,
By the touch of God's own love.

Is to ban-ish ev-'ry fear; As we reach to touch His hand. He our

hearts will un-der-stand; He will hold us, He will guide, He will keep us

by His side, Thro' the night and thro' the day, On thro' all e - ter-ni - ty.

No. 21. SWEET DREAMS OF LONG AGO.

LAURA E. NEWELL.
Duet.

J. F. KING.

Moderato.

1. There's a dream that fond mem-'ry still will cher - ish,
2. By the mill where as chil-dren oft we'd wan - der,
3. But 'tis past, all the trans-port of our child - hood,

As life's tides ebb and si - lent - ly flow; Tho' blos-soms of sum-
When our school and its tasks were for - got; The church by the glen
We life's cares and its tri - als must know; Yet scenes of those days

mer may per - ish, Still a - bide tho'ts of dear long a - go.
o - ver yon - der, Dear to us, still that calm hallowed spot.
in the wild - wood Live in hearts; blest the sweet long a - go.

CHORUS.

Sweet dreams of the past

Oh! come, come, come, come, come, sweet dreams, come, come, come, come,

still we'll cher - ish O'er life thro' a bright gold - en

come, come, come, come, come, come, come, come, come,

Sweet Dreams of Long Ago.—Concluded.

glow;

p

come, oh, come, Fond vis - ions of youth nev - er per - ish,

f   **Rit. and Dim.**

Bliss - ful dreams of the sweet long a - go, (long a - go.)

No. 22.   **BED-TIME, KATE! (Round.)**

J. M. DUNGAN.

When you go a - court - ing, Do not stay too late,

Lest you hear the voice of ma - ma, Say-ing, "Bed-time, Kate!"

No. 23.   **HATS. (Round.)**

J. T. REESE.

Hats, hats, nice new hats! Hats, hats, tip, top hats!

Soft hats, stiff hats, fine fur hats! Straw hats, wool hats, stove pipe hats!

No. 24. NO MATTER WHAT OTHER FOLKS DO.

LAURA E. NEWELL.

CHRISTIAN J. KING.

1. Stand firm in the right, do not quail And falter when tempted to wrong,
2. Don't stumble o'er faults of a friend, Be onward and upward, your way;
3. Look up! wear a brave smiling face; Be patient, and earnest, and true;

For *right* must with heroes prevail, And hearts must be fearless and strong.
Tho' storms may in fury de-scend, Clouds will not obscure all the day.
You'll win at the end of the race, No matter what other folks do.

CHORUS.

No matter what other folks do, Be gen-u-ine, loy-al and true;

Be honest and kind, Serene keep your mind, No matter what other folks do.

WHISTLE AND BE GAY.

J. M. F.

J. H. Fillmore.

Cheerful.

1. I am full of fun and glee, And as hap-py as can be. For I'm
2. I a - rise at peep of day, And try al-ways to be gay, For I
3. O I am a jo-vial lad, With a heart that's never sad, And I

al-ways bright and cheerful, as you see ; For I whistle all the day In a
whistle whether at my work or play; All my friends and schoolmates dear, To each
whistle, for I always feel so glad ; For in sunshine and in rain, Hear me

glad and joy-ous way, As I try to do my du - ty and be gay.
one I bring good cheer, As they hear my merry whistle loud and clear.
whistle clear and plain, While the hill-sides echo back the glad re-frain.

Whistling Duet.

1

2 *3*

No. 26. KEEP ON SINGING.

Laura E. Newell. Christian J. King.

Moderato.

1. Life may prove a thorn-y way, Keep on singing! Keep on singing!
2. True, some heavy burdens fall, Keep on singing! Keep on singing!
3. Cast your burdens on the Lord. Keep on singing! Keep on singing!

You're advancing day by day, Keep on singing! Keep on singing!
On you, but they hin-der all, Keep on singing! Keep on singing!
Peace you'll find is your re-ward, Keep on singing! Keep on singing!

And the tri-als that you meet Sure-ly, swift-ly you'll de - feat
Cher-ish still this humble thought, "If we strive, as strive we ought,
In your heart so true and strong, Foster hope's ex - ul-tant song,

If you'll trust with faith complete Keep on singing! Keep on singing!
Efforts will not come to nought." Keep on singing! Keep on singing!
Lo, the journey is not long! Keep on singing! Keep on singing!

No. 27. BELLS OF CHRISTMAS.

Laura E. Newell.

J. M. Dungan.

1. Don't you hear the sleigh-bells jin - gle, Jin - gle, jin - gle on the air?
2. We can al - most hear him laughing, For a jol - ly one is he;
3. Mer-ry Christmas! mer - ry Christmas! 'Tis the crowning of the year

While the rein-deer and Kris Krin-gle Are ex - pect - ed ev - 'ry-where,
Who is nev - er, nev - er sulk - ing, But is o - ver-stocked with glee;
Wel-come, wel-come, fes - tive sea - son, With its mirth and wealth of cheer;

He is com - ing! sure - ly com - ing With an ex - tra lot of toys,
Lis - ten! don't you hear him sing-ing? On the chimney keep an eye,
And we hear the sweetest message, Peace on earth, good-will t'ward men,

Cho.—He is com-ing! com-ing! com-ing! Don't you hear him on the way?

That he will dis - tri - bute on - ly Just a- mong good girls and boys.
When the bells are mad - ly ring-ing Sure - ly he must be near by.
When the Christmas bells are ring-ing, Peal-ing forth their notes a - gain.

D. S. for Chorus.

O, his sleigh-bells mer - ry jin - gle Gladdens hearts this Christmas day.

No. 28.   THE FARMER BOY.

LAURA E. NEWELL.

J. T. REESE.

Cheerful.

1 Oh! the cit - y oft may al - lure man - kind, With its
2. There's a smile for him in each op' - ning flow'r, And the
3. Not a - fraid of toil! not a shirk is he. Strong of
4 Here's to him who no - bly per - forms his part, And in

pleas - ures mixed with a vain al - loy, But for peace se - rene,
songs of birds are a con - stant joy; While some new de - light
hand and heart, work may nev - er c oy Him whose worth we sing,
wor - thy aims doth his time em - ploy, Heav - en bless the lad

and a stead - fast mind, View the mer - ry farm - er boy.
ev - 'ry live - long hour Greets our earn - est farm - er boy.
gen - ial, brave and free Is our hap - py farm - er boy.
with a sun - ny heart, Bless our faith - ful farm - er boy!

CHORUS.

Oh! he whis - tles, Gai - ly

Oh! he whis - tles, gai - ly whis - tles, Or he

The Farmer Boy.—Concluded.

whis - tles,

hums a live - ly tune, As light - heart - ed to his

ne goes, Tra, la,

la - bor now he goes, he goes ; Tra, la,

la, la, Tra, la, la, la,

la, la, la, la, la, Mer - ry as the birds of June,

Is our farm - er lad 'mid na - ture's sweet re - pose.

No. 29.   IT ALL COMES BACK TO ME AGAIN.

LAURA E. NEWELL.   J. F. KING.

Moderato.

1. It all comes back to me a - gain, That sum - mer by the
2. It all comes back to me a - gain, The sto - ry ev - er
3. It all comes back to me a - gain, The past I'll ne'er for-

sea,   Its change - ful scenes I now re - view,   So
new.   You breathed to me be - neath the stars,   My
get.   Those sun - ny days be - side the sea,   With-

dear to mem - o - ry,   The years may come, and years may
love so fond and true;   We did not know the fu - ture
out one sad re - gret,   E'en then the reap - er was as

go,   While bides life's sad re - frain,   But none as
then, 'Twas hid - den from our sight,   But we'll re-
near, That all my hopes hath slain,   And you are

It All Comes Back to Me Again.—Concluded.

bright, my heart may know Can come to me a - gain.
new those sa - cred vows Be - yond the tears; and night.
gone, and I am here, It all comes back a - gain.

CHORUS.

a tempo.

It all comes back to me a - gain, That

f   *Cres*

sum - mer by the sea, Its gold - en hours I now re -

f   *Rit and Dim.*

call, So dear to mem - o - ry, (to mem - o - ry.)

HAPPY CHILDHOOD.

T. F. F.   T. F. FRANCIS.

1. Oh, the hap - py hours of child-hood, But how soon they pass a - way,
2. Now re - mem- ber you can nev - er   Live your childhood o'er a - gain,
3. Then the cares of life will meet you At each cor - ner of its stage,

Like the lit - tle danc-ing sun-beams Of a bright and sun-ny day.
For the girls will soon be wo - men, And the boys will soon be men.
Write them down, and let your re - cord Have no blot on eith - er page.

CHORUS.

Then im - prove............ the pass-ing   moments,

Then im-prove the pass-ing moments, Then im-prove the passing moments.

For they nev - - - - er will re - turn;............

For they nev - er will re-turn,   For they nev-er will re-turn:

And your lives .... will all be

And your lives will all be meas - ured, And your

measured

lives will all be measured By the things in youth you learn.

No. 31. LITTLE WHITE LILY.

GEO. McDONALD.

B. F. STUBER.

Moderato.

Cres - - - -

1 Li-ly, white li-ly, sat by a stone, Drooping and waiting till the sun shone,
2 Little white lily said: "It is good:" Lit-tle white li-ly's clothing and food;
3 Little white li-ly, drooping with pain, Waiting and waiting for the wet rain;
4. Little white li-ly smells very sweet; On her head sunshine, rain at her feet.

Rit. - - - -

Little white li-ly sunshine has fed; Little white li-ly is lift-ing her head.
Little white lily dressed like a bride, Shining like whiteness and crowned beside!
Little white li-ly holding her cup; Rain is fast falling and filling it up.
Thanks to the sunshine, thanks to the rain, Little white li-ly is happy a-gain,

HAIL COLUMBIA!

G. W. F.

G. W. FIELDS.

With Vigor.

1. Hail Co-lum-bia! Grand old un-ion, Freedom's banner waves on high;
2. Hail Co-lum-bia! 'Twas our fathers Suffered, for what we en-joy;
3. Hail Co-lum-bia! Teach the children, Loy-al-ty to our fair land;

All the world will learn to know thee, Lib-er-ty, all freemen cry.
We will suf-fer to maintain thee, For we are "Co-lum-bia's" boy.
Teach them that the home of free-dom Is our own "Co-lum-bia" grand.

Cres.

CHORUS.

Hail, Co-lum-bia! All u-nit-ed, Grandest na-tion of the world;

All can see and Know our mot-to, Freedom's banner is un-furled.

No. 33.   BOB WHITE.

Lulu Dilley Donica.   J. F. King.

1. Up-on a fence in the mead-ow A bird sat sing-ing a
2. His mod-est mate was sit-ing Up-on her treas-ures
3. "Oh, tell me, lit-tle whist-ler, Why are you al-ways

song, From ear-ly morn till late in the eve, And nev-er a
wee; And tho' no note she whis-tled, Her heart was
gay?" And tho' I asked him of-ten, These words were

note went wrong.
full of glee.
all he'd say.

CHORUS. f

Bob White! Bob White!
Bob White! Bob White!

He whis-tled loud and clear.
The (Omit ....)   name to him so dear.

Repeat Chorus pp.

* Tenor and Bass may whistle their parts, if preferred.

COME AWAY.

T. B. W.

T B. WEAVER.

With spirit.

1. Come a-way,...... come a-way,...... Oh, come with a
   Come a-way, come a-way,
2. Come a-way,...... come a-way,...... Oh, let us for-

heart light and gay! ...... Come a-way, ... come a-way, ...
   Come a-way, come a-way,
sake all our care,...... Come a-way,...... come a-way,......

light and gay,
all our care.

Come join in the mirth of the day; Come a-way, ... come a-
   Come a-way,
All na-ture is glad ev-'ry-where, Come a-way, ... come a-

way,...... Let sor-row and care not an-noy,...... Ban-ish all
come a-way,
way, ... Let du-ties and toil not an-noy,...... Ban-ish all

not an-noy,

Come Away.—Concluded.

sad-ness, and cherish all gladness, Oh, come with a heart full of joy.

CHORUS.—*WALTZ.*

Come out in the meadows so green; Come,

La, la, la, la, la, la, la, La, la,

Tra, Tra, Tra, la, la, la, Tra,

row on the wa-ters se - rene; Come, rest in the

La, la, la, la, la, la, la, la, la, la,

Tra, Tra, la, la, la, Tra, Tra,

cool, qui - et bow'rs; *Rit.* *Repeat pp*

la, la, la, Come with the birds and the flowers.

oh, come!

Tra. la, la, la

SNOWFLAKES.

LULU DILLEY DONICA.   D. E. KING.

1. Out of the depths of the heaven;   Out of the lim - it - less space;
2. That which was old is now hidden; New forms are brought into view:

Out of the bound - less o - cean,   Out from un-der God's face.
Snowflakes are mes-sa-ges sent us— Mes-sa-ges boundless and true,—

O - ver the meadows and woodlands, O-ver the earth brown and bare,
God's love will cov-er our weakness; God's love will les-sen our woe;

Cov - er - ing all with a man - tle   Spot - less and fair.
God's love will make pure and spot - less Just as the snow.

Snowflakes.—Concluded.

CHORUS.

Beau-ti-ful snow-flakes are fall-ing, Fall-ing from heaven a-bove;

Beau-ti-ful, beau-ti-ful snow-flakes, Tell-ing of God and His love.

No. 36. SINGING.

Words Selected.

Lively.

B. F. STUBER.

1. Of speckled eggs the birdie sings, And nests among the trees ; . . . .
   D.S.—The sailor sings of ropes and things, In ships upon the . . . seas.
2. The children sing in far Japan, The children sing in Spain; . . , . .
   D.S.—The or-gan, with the organ-man, Is sing-ing in the . . . . rain.

CHORUS.

D.S. 2d ending.
a tempo.

Tra la . . . la la, ... Tra la . . . . la la. . . . . The
la la   la la,   la la   la la. The

No. 37. THE SUNSHINE IN A SMILE.

Lizzie A. Switzer.   G. W. Fields.

Put sunshine into your face.

1. There is naught in art so charm-ing As the sun-shine
2. When the face is bright and shin-ing, It can chase the
3. Let the face light up in smil-ing, All the way from

of a smile; There is noth-ing so dis-arm-ing, To the
gloom a-way, All the deep drawn frowns be-guil-ing, In-to
brow to chin, And think not, they be de-fil-ing, If some

poig-nant point of trial; If you smile, the world will
smiles, like sun-beams play, For an-oth-er's face will
peo-ple say you grin, Ra-diant glow, like sun-light

bright-en, It will an-swer back a-gain, And the
mir-ror, All our pleas-ure or our pain, Let us
shin-ing, On the mountains capped with snow, Which the

The Sunshine in a Smile.—Concluded.

load will seem to light-en, We are stronger now than then.
bind them to us near-er, By the sun-shine, not the rain.
In-dians, wild, de-fin-ing, Called the brightness, I-da-ho.

CHORUS.

Oh, the sun - shine,
Sun-shine, sun-shine of a smile, When it,
Oh, the sun - shine,

Cres. - - - - -
like the sun-beams play; Sun-shine, sun-shine,
Oh, the sun - shine, Oh, the sun - shine,

of a smile, How it drives all gloom a - way.

No. 38, THE GOLDEN RULE.

T. B. W.

T. B. WEAVER.

Solo.

1. In our school, we should endeavor The golden rule to learn;—
2. As we journey 'long life's path-way, And meet with fa-ces new,
3. A deed of true com-pas-sion Is nev-er lost for aye;

Cres. - - - - -

To do to oth-ers as we wish That they'd do in re-turn.
We'll try to keep this gold-en rule, As on-ward we pur-sue.
For lov-ing hands will do the same For you in some kind way.

A word thus kind-ly spo-ken, A deed thus no-bly done,
We'll scat-ter seeds of kind-ness, Wher-ev-er we may go,
A smile to cheer some lone one, A rose bestowed in tears,

Will tru-ly bring a sure re-ward Of joy to ev-'ry one.
While bless-ing oth-ers we'll be blessed, And sweeter life will grow.
Will bring you man-y days of joy, And li-lies, af-ter years.

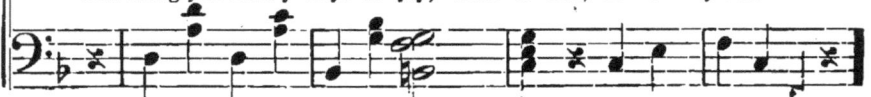

From NATURE SONGS. Laning Printing Co. Norwalk. O.

The Golden Rule.—Concluded.

CHORUS.

Do un - to oth - ers as you wish they'd do to you;

Do un - to oth - ers as you wish they'd do to you.

Do un - to oth - ers as you wish they'd do to you;

And thus ful - fill the gold - en rule at school.

No. 39. MY DEAR OLD HOME.

LUELLA D. STILLMAN.

W. O. CARROLL.

Moderato.

m

1. Oh, the dear old home on the hill - side, How near it seemed
2. Oh, the dear old home on the hill - side, Where my ear - ly

to the sky, When I used to watch, at e - ven - tide, The
days were spent! My heart, as light as the this - tle down, Knew

Cres.   *m*   *f*

white clouds sail - ing by; Out un - der the spreading elm tree,
naught of dis - con - tent; I have tast-ed earth's gay pleas - ures,

m   *f*

In the clov - er fresh and sweet, With Rov - er, my
And found them emp - ty and vain, And yearn for the

My Dear Old Home.—Concluded.

trust - ed play - mate, Romp - ing there at my feet.
child - hood fan - cies And child - like faith a - gain.

CHORUS.

Oh, my dear old home! My hap - py
dear old home! hap - py home!

child-hood home! Oh, my dear old
hap - py child - hood home! dear old hap - py

home! My dear old hap - py child - hood home!
child - hood home!

No. 40. OUR FLAG.

Lizzie A. Switzer.   G. W. Fields.

Lively.

1. We hail the en-sign of the free, The stars on field of blue;
2. Our U-nion great, U - ni-ted States, With freedom's flag en-twined;

Its col - ors rare, the no - ble three, The red, the white, the blue.
Oh, sis - ter states! what-e'er a - waits, Our flag shall ev - er bind.

f   *m*

Our en-sign bright, dis-pels the night, And floats in triumph for the
With col - ors three, flag of the free, Our pride on land, our pride on

right, A flag of might, with col - ors bright, The red, the white, the blue.
sea, May hon-or, bright, un-tarn-ished be, She'll nev-er be be-hind!

No. 41. A MERRY FARMER'S BOY.

1. A mer - ry farmer's boy am I, And my songs are gay and blithe;
2. The chatt'ring squirrel welcomes me, As I light-ly trip a - long,
3. Then let me live a farmer's life, Nor chide me for my wish;

For in my hum - ble coun-try home, I lead a glad free life.
And bird, and bees, and I u - nite, To sing a joy - ful song.
For o - ver all the wide, wide world, There is no life like this.

CHORUS.

Oh, I'm a mer - ry farm-er's boy, Farmer's boy, farmer's boy;

Repeat pp.

Oh, I'm a mer - ry farm-er's boy, A mer - ry farm-er's boy.

No. 42.

SLEIGHING.

Lizzie A. Switzer.

G. W. Fields.

Allegro.

1. O'er glist'ning snow we swift - ly glide, Our po - nies
2. In mer - ry mood we on - ward sweep, The night's too
3. Such hap - py times, light hearts may know, The bells' sweet

go, they're true and tried; The twink - ling stars are
good to spend in sleep; With joy and health, a
chimes in mu - sic flow; The joy - ous laugh is

bright and fair, The moon - lit bars their glo - ry share.
mer - ry band, We have a wealth that tests will stand.
sweet and clear, Fond pleas - ures quaff with friends most dear.

CHORUS.

Hear the jin - gle, jin - gle, jin - gle, O'er the

Sleighing.—Concluded.

snow we glide, To the mer - ry, mer - ry, mer - ry, mer - ry jin - gle of the bells; Oh, the jin - gle, jin - gle,

Cres. ....

jin - gle, jin - gle, jin - gle, jin - gle, jin - gle, jin - gle,

Ac - *cel* - *er* - - *an*-

f *áo.*   *ff*   *Repeat pp.*

jin - gle, jin - gle, jin - gle, jin - gle, jin - gle of the bells.

No. 43. DON'T TAKE IT TO HEART.

LAURA E. NEWELL.

JOHN McPHERSON.

1. As you jour-ney ev - er on-ward Thro' this "vale of tears,"
2. There are man-y kinds of peo-ple Who com-pose this globe,
3. But no mat-ter, do not wor-ry, Go right straight a - head;

If you'd bless the world where-ev - er you may go,
Good and bad, and some in - dif - fer - ent, we find;
Do not ev - er search for trou - ble, no ! no ! ! no ! ! !

Just be cheer - ful, though are lag - ging Oft the change-ful
Those who help you, those who hin - der, Those who seek to
Wake the ech - oes with your mu - sic, It has well been

years; Be a sun - beam, and send out a
probe, Ev - 'ry se - cret, with an all too
said. We shall reap in - deed what - ev - er

Don't Take It to Heart.—Concluded.

gen - ial glow.
read - y mind.
we may sow.   Don't take it to heart,

Don't take it to heart, The word that was

thought-less - ly said; Just laugh off your care, And

nev - er des - pair, Tho' rug - ged the path - way you tread.

No. 44. GOOD NIGHT.

J. H. F.

Slow.

J. H. Fillmore.

1. Good night, good night, To one and all good night, The
2. Good night, good night, To one and all good night, We're
3. Good night, good night, To one and all good night, And

time has come when we must say, To one and all a kind good night.
glad to have your presence here, And may our sing-ing bring good cheer.
should we nev-er meet a-gain On earth, we hope to meet in heav'n.

CHORUS.

Rit. e dim.

Repeat pp.

Good night, good night, good night, good night.
good night, good night, good night.

INDEX.

❦ ❦ ❦

www.ingramcontent.com/pod-product-compliance
Lightning Source LLC
Chambersburg PA
CBHW030613270326
41927CB00007B/1149